Bonnie Raitt

Longing In Their Hearts

Edited by Milton Okun

Management: Ron Stone and Jeffrey Hersh for Gold Mountain Entertainment
Piano/Vocal Arrangements by Edwin McLean
Music Engraving by Edwin McLean
Production: Daniel Rosenbaum/Rana Bernhardt
Art Direction: Rosemary Cappa-Jenkins
Director of Music: Mark Phillips

Photography: Cover, pp. 2, 3, 57 by John Casado, courtesy Capitol Records.
Pp. 15, 29 by Robert Zuckerman.
Cover logotype and lettering by Tim Girvin Design, Inc., courtesy Capitol Records.

• *Cherry Lane gratefully acknowledges Andy Stoller for his help in the preparation of this book.*

Contents

Love Sneakin' Up On You

Words and Music by
Jimmy Scott and Tom Snow

F♯7
Tell me now, I've got to know, do you feel the same?
A7
Do you just light up at the men - tion of my name?
Chorus
D
Don't wor - ry, ba - by, it ain't noth - in' new;
Bm7
that's just love sneak - in'
C
up on you. If your
D
whole world is shak - in', and you feel like I do,

Bm7
1. C
that's just love sneak - in' up on you.
D
2. C
up on you.
D
C
G
F
D
C
G
F#7
A7

Additional Lyrics

2. Nowhere on earth for your heart to hide
Once love comes sneakin' up on your blind side.
And you might as well try to stop the rain
Or stand in the tracks of a runaway train.
You just can't fight it when a thing is meant to be,
Come on, let's finish what you started with me. *(To Chorus)*

Longing In Their Hearts

Words by Michael O'Keefe
Music by Bonnie Raitt

D
E
A
spice. He reads his cus - to - mers like a book.
Asus4
A
E
A
He's seen this and he's done that, and now he's mak - in' fried eggs an art.
D
E
But there's one thing he can't
A
D
1. E
A
fix no - how; there's a long - ing in his heart.
Asus4
A
E
A
Asus4
A

2.
E
Chorus
A
E/A
house un-der a big sky. Well, e - ven the stars at night
D/A
A
A/C♯
D
a - gree that the sky is fall - ing a - part.
E
A
She knows 'cause she can feel it too.
D
E
A
There is a long - ing in her heart,
Asus4
A
E
A
Asus4
A
a long-ing in her heart,

E
To Coda
A
long - ing in her heart.
G
D/F♯
D
A/C♯
Well, you and me, we're just like them; we nev - er
B7
want - ed to be a - lone.
So we made
A
D
a pact, sealed with de - sire,
E
for a hap - pi - er house and home,

G
D/F♯
D
A/C♯
on - ly to find it does - n't un - tie the knot where feel-ings die.
B7
A
There's a long - ing deep in - side
D
our hearts, and
E
A
E
A
no one to tell us why.
Asus4
A
E

A7
D
A7
D
D.S. (take 2nd ending) al Coda
3. Well,
Coda
A7

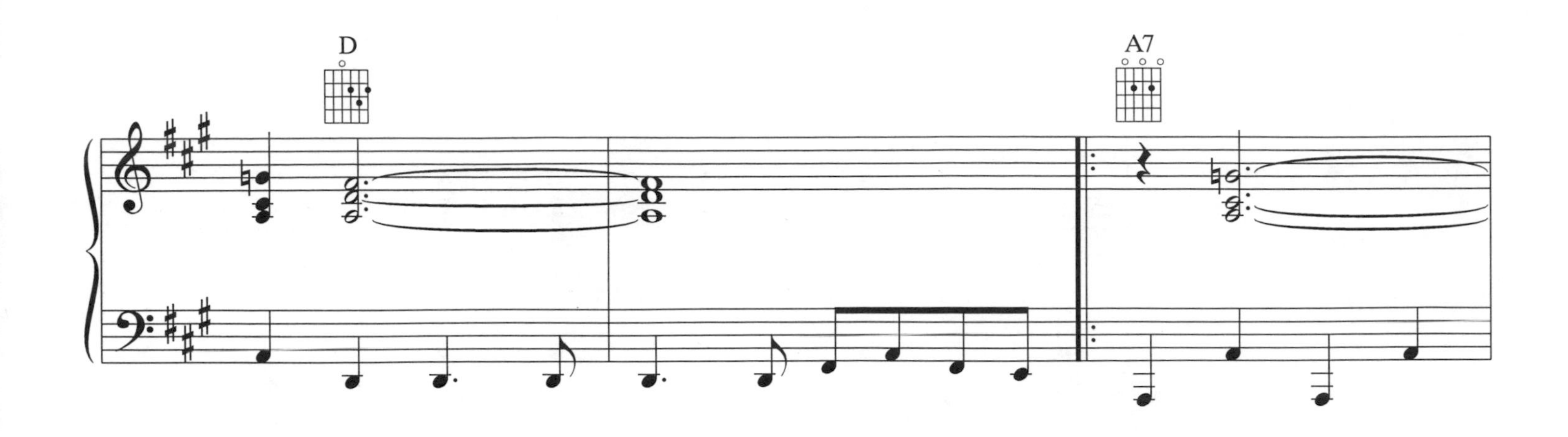

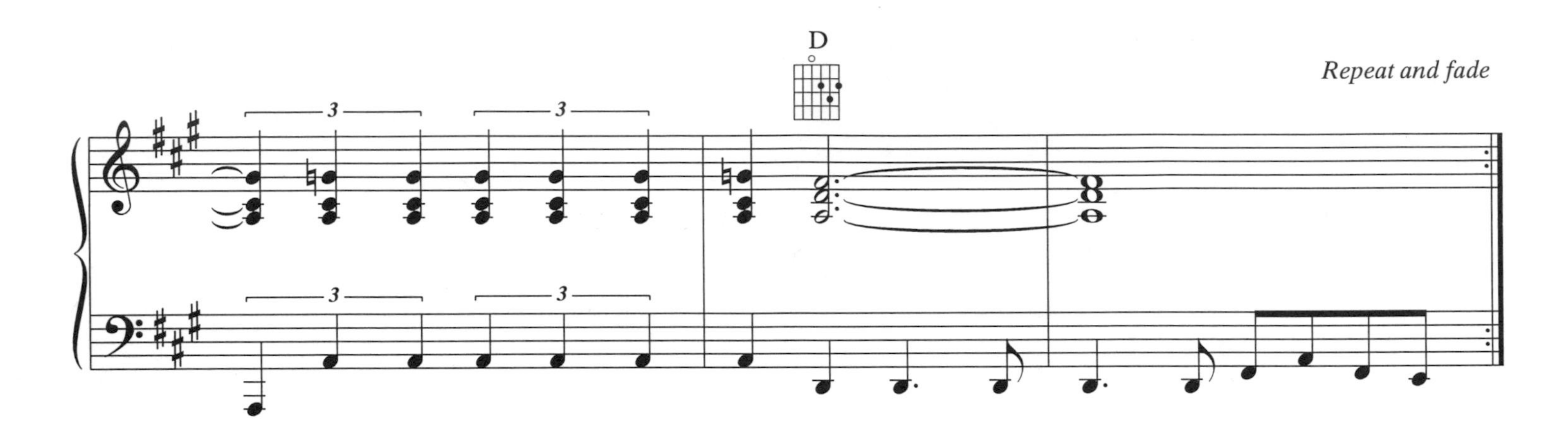

Additional Lyrics

2. He's tried for years to work it out
At the grill and at his home.
Well, he talks to his friends, talks to himself;
He talks the chicken right off the bone.
Talks to his woman and she understands;
You know they're always eye to eye.
She runs the joint; they live out back,
Small house under a big sky. *(To Chorus)*

3. Well, our friends aren't looking for anything new;
They wouldn't know where to look.
Well her, she likes running the joint,
And he likes being a cook.
Together they're doing very well;
They're mighty glad they could.
But there's a fire burning towards them now,
Coming from a distant wood.

2nd Chorus:
And even the stars at night agree
That the sky is falling apart.
We know 'cause we can feel it too;
There's a longing in our hearts,
Longing in our hearts,
Longing in our hearts.

You

Words and Music by
Bob Thiele, Jr., Steven Krikorian
and John Shanks

B
A
You were the on - ly one that mat -
Was - n't that love that we were feel -
E
C♯m
4fr.
tered.
ing. (That was something, baby.)
Then you were gone;
Deep in our soul,
E
love had moved on,
deep - er than we know,
A
left me a - lone, think-ing of
keep - ing me hold - ing out for

B
E
A
you. There was nev - er an - y oth - er.
you. There was nev - er an - y ques - tion.
B
E
You and I were cre - at - ed to be true.
You'll be for - ev - er on my mind.
Asus2
E/G♯
1.
F♯m7add4
E
2.
F♯m7add4
E
B
E
You and I, we were meant to be to - geth -
A
B
er.
True hearts in a world

E
Asus2
E/G♯
F♯m7add4
E
where love is dy - in'.
D
A
D
I might as well have been dy - in' when we were a - part.
F♯m
B
E
When you came back, I felt the beat -
3
Asus2
E/G♯
F♯m7add4
E
ing of my heart.
B
E
A

B
E
Asus2
E/G♯
F♯m7add4
E
B
E
A
You and I, there was nev - er an - y ques- tion.
B
E
You'll be for - ev - er on my mind.
Asus2
E/G♯
F♯m7add4
E
B
You and I, we were meant

E
A
to be together.
B
E
Asus2
E/G♯
You...
F♯m7add4
E
B
E
It was always you.
A
B
Always you.
E
Asus2
E/G♯
F♯m7add4
E
Repeat and fade

Cool, Clear Water

Words and Music by
Bonnie Raitt

A
E
D/F♯
E/G♯
Feel my earth turn o - ver, dar-lin', till I'm root-less and un - bound.
A
Asus4
A
Asus4
E
I want to feel my bod - y trem-
F♯m
E/G♯
A
Asus4
ble when there's no one else a-round.
Verse 3 only: Play this measure twice
A
Asus4
A
E7sus4
Just this cool clear wa - ter run-nin'

To Coda
1. D
E
A
in this love that I've found.
Hey ba -
D
E
A
D
E
by, see how it feels
ev - 'ry time you re -
F♯m
D
E7sus4
veal your - self to me.
I'll come run - nin'.
A
D
E
A
D
E
2. I want to feel

2. A
D
E
A
D
E7sus4
me.
Hey,
ba- by.
D/E
A/E
E
1. All
2. Instrumental ad lib
my life
I
have
known
there's
some- thing more,
D/E
A/E
love
to
blind
me
like
E
D/E
the sun.
Deep

A/E
E
in dreams I will wash up on your shore.
D/E
A/E
E
Now I know that you're the one.
1.
2.
E7sus4
D
E
A
D
E
A
D
E

F♯m7
D
E7sus4
A
D
E
A
D
E
D.S. al Coda
3. And when I feel
Coda
A
D
E
A
D
am.
Hey,
ba - by.
E
A
D
E
We'll be all
right
all
the

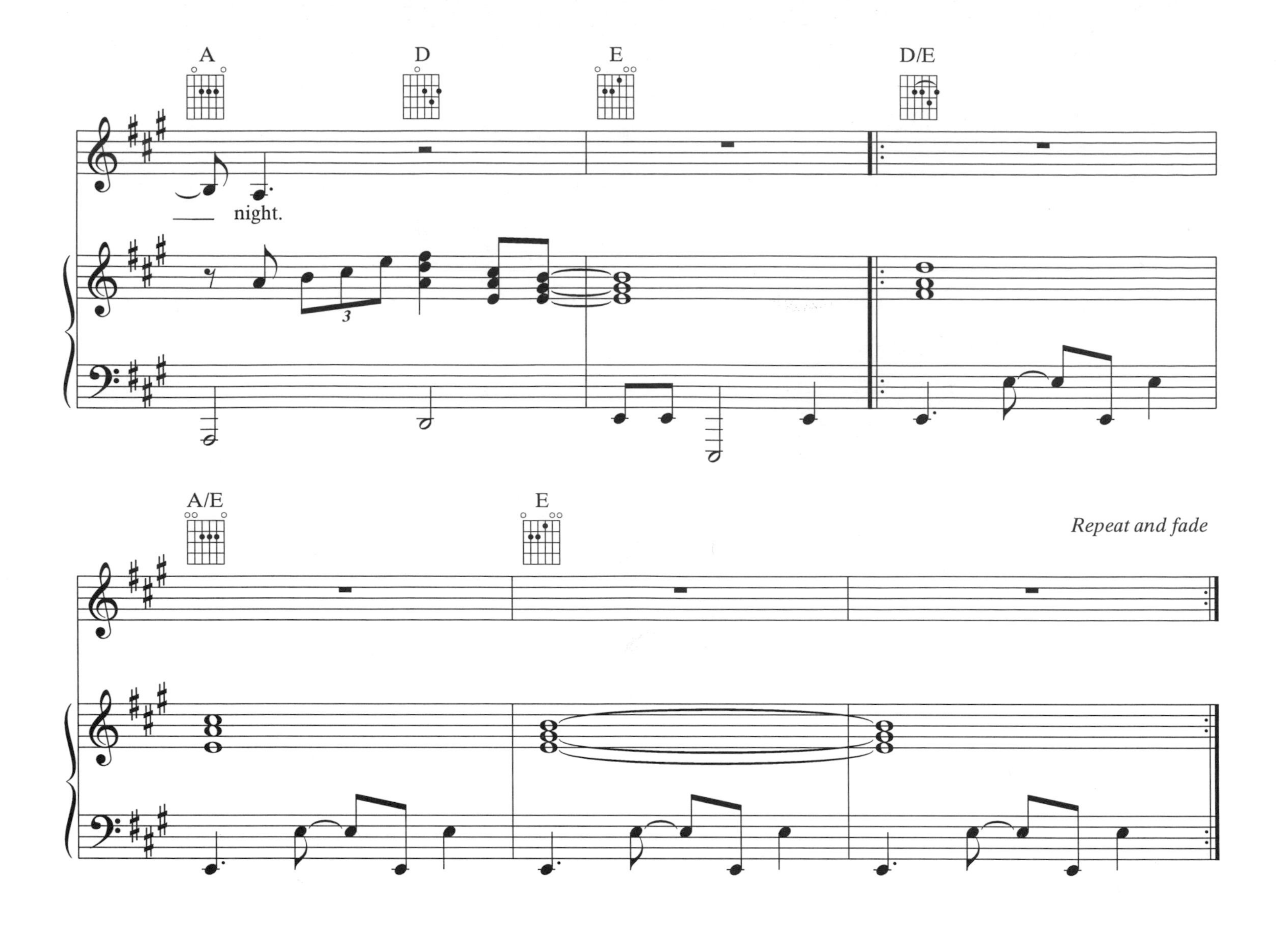

Additional Lyrics

2. I want to feel myself go under, baby,
   Where the deepest river bleeds.
   I want to feel it pull me under, darlin',
   Until it drops me to my knees.
   I want to know that I can find you
   When there's no more eyes to see.
   In this cool, clear water runnin',
   You'll come runnin' to me.

3. And when I feel my baby callin',
   It's like a whisper in the sand.
   When the softest rain is fallin', darlin',
   I will crumble in your hand.
   Then when all that's left is wonder,
   And no need to understand,
   Well, this cool, clear water runnin'
   Will be all that I am.

CIRCLE DANCE

Words and Music by
Bonnie Raitt

2nd time: A
Bm
D
G
A
Worn out steps from long a - go
Em7
D
D/F♯
G
Asus4
A
don't give love a chance.
It's
D/F♯
G
A
a bit - ter heir - loom hand - ed down,
D/F♯
G
Asus4
A
these twist - ed parts we play.
D
G
A
Bm
I'm not her and you're not him;

Em7
D/F♯
Asus4
A
just comes out that way.
Chorus
G
A
G/B
A/C♯
Can't go back to make things right though I
wish I'd un - der - stood.
Time has made things clear - er now;
1.2.
Em7
we did the best we could.

Additional Lyrics

2. "I'll be home soon," that's what you'd say,
   And a little kid believes.
   After a while I learned that love
   Must be a thing that leaves.
   I tried so hard just to hold you near,
   Was as good as I could be.
   Even when I had you here.
   You stayed so far from me.

   2nd Chorus:
   Can't go back to make things right,
   Though I wish I'd understood.
   Time has made things clearer now;
   You did the best you could.

3. *Instrumental (8 bars)*
   Now that this has occurred to me,
   But I wanted you to know:
   I've been too faithful all my life;
   It's time to let you go. *(To Chorus)*

   3rd Chorus:
   Instrumental (4 bars)
   Time has made things clearer now. *etc.*

I Sho Do

Words and Music by
Mabon "Teenie" Hodges and Billy Always

D7
A7
but you weren't giv - ing up, ba - by, what you should.
Chorus
D7
A7
D7
A7
I sho do need you. I sho do
1.
2.
D7
A7
want you. want you. I sho do
D7
A7
wish for you. I sho do walk the floor all night long.

Bm7
Em7
When you see me, ba - by, stand - ing a- lone,
Bm7
Em7
come and help me, ba - by, 'cause I'm out here on my own.
Bm7
Em7
You see it ain't eas - y in the streets,
E7
F♯7
but what you got, ba - by, it could help me to my feet, yeah.

Additional Lyrics

2. I'm in need of what you've got;
It makes my blood boiling hot.
You told me, baby, a long time ago
That you'd never, ever leave me,
Never, no more. *(To Chorus)*

DIMMING OF THE DAY

Words and Music by
Richard Thompson

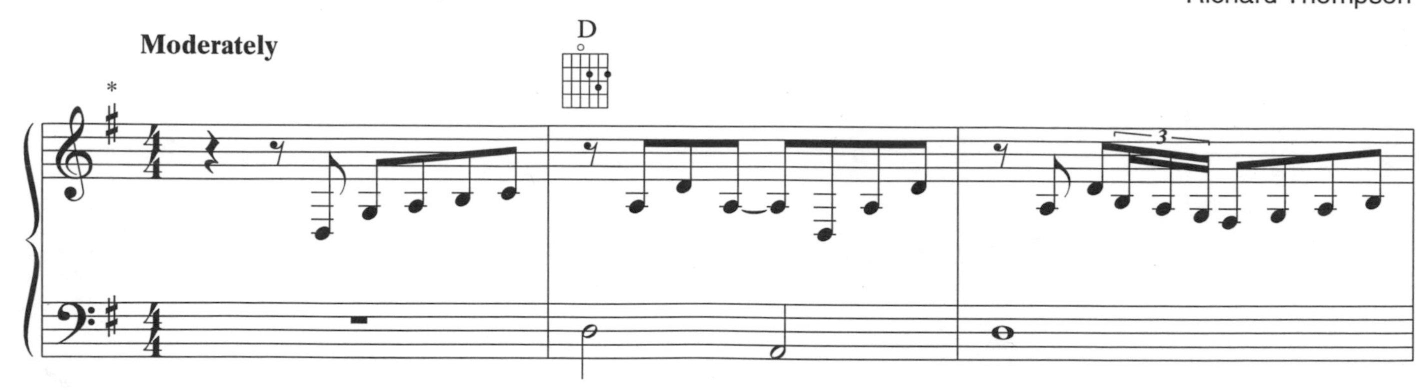

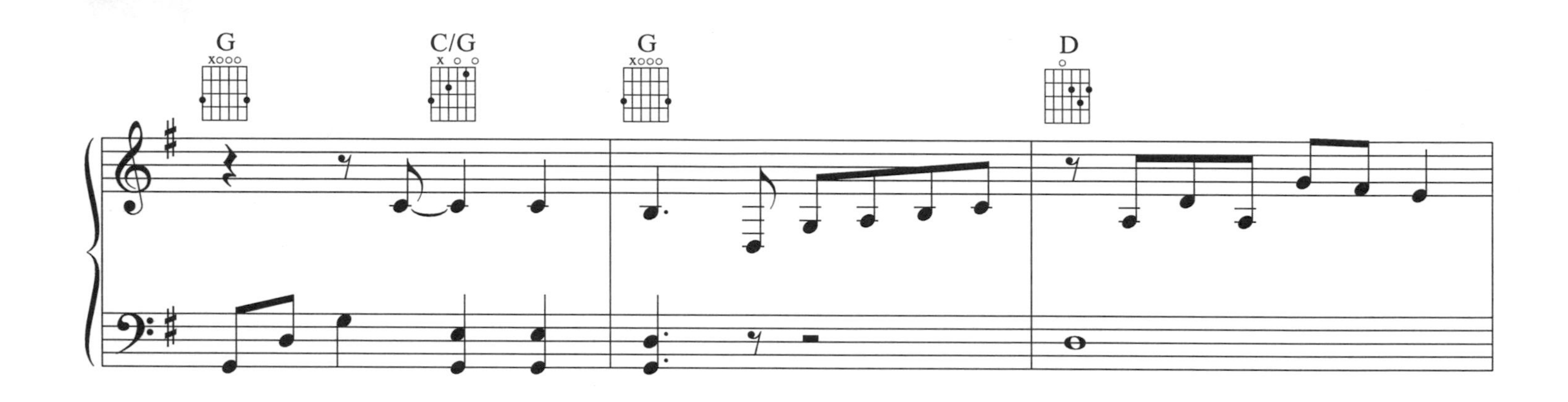

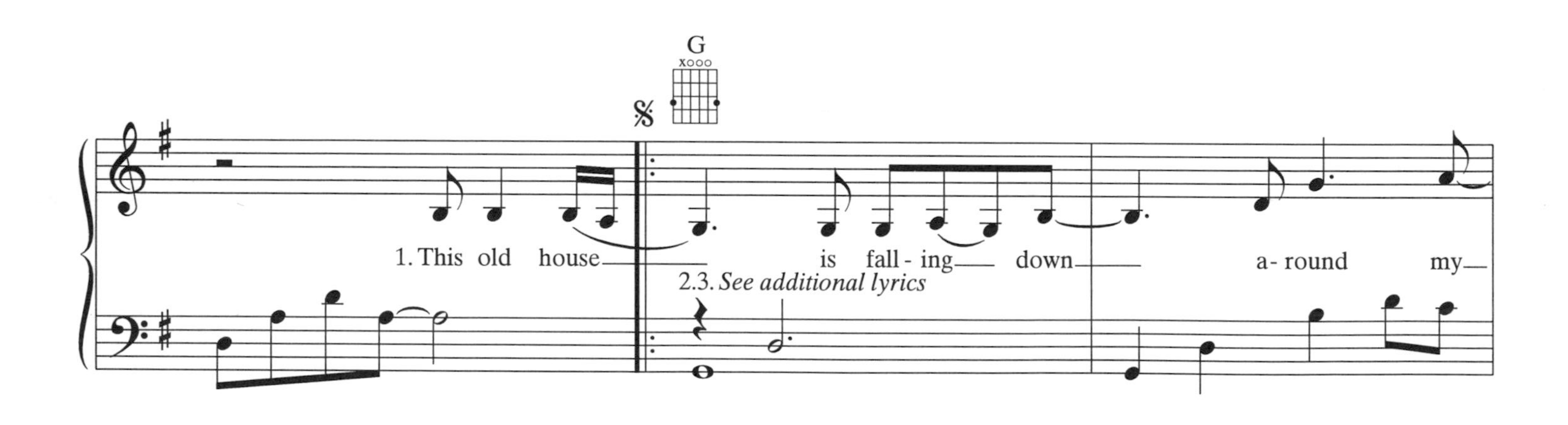

* Recorded a half step higher.

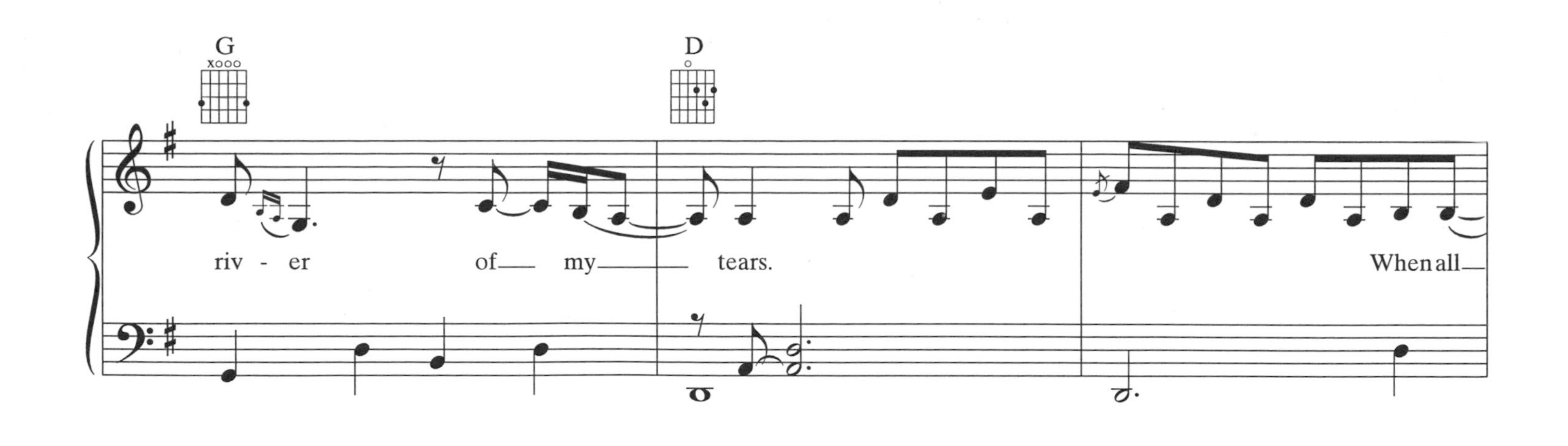
G
D
riv - er of my tears. When all

G
D
my will is gone, you hold me sway

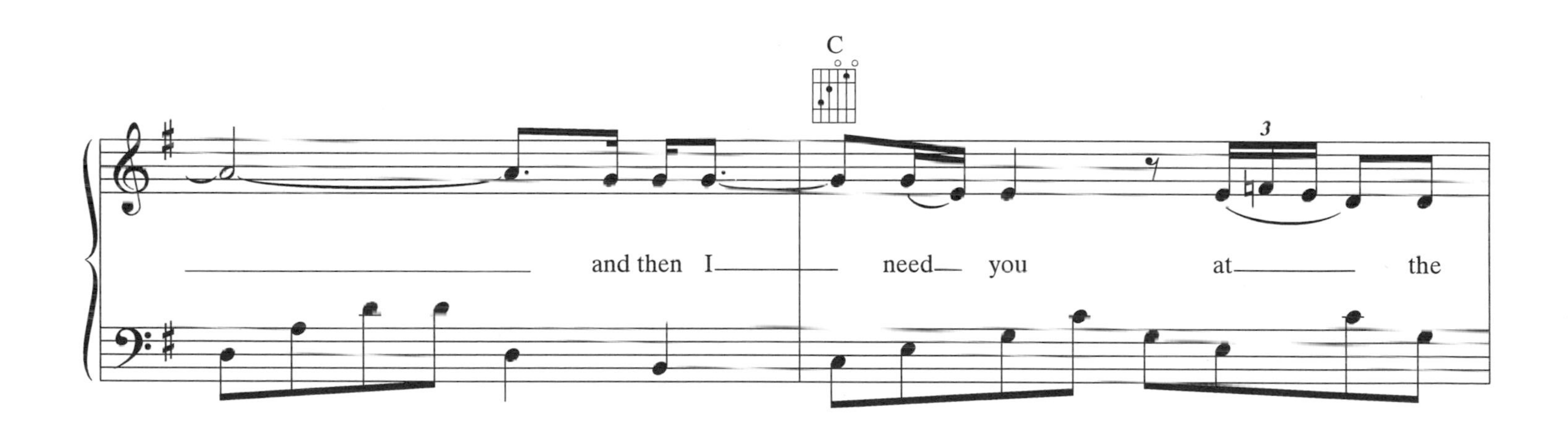
C
3
and then I need you at the

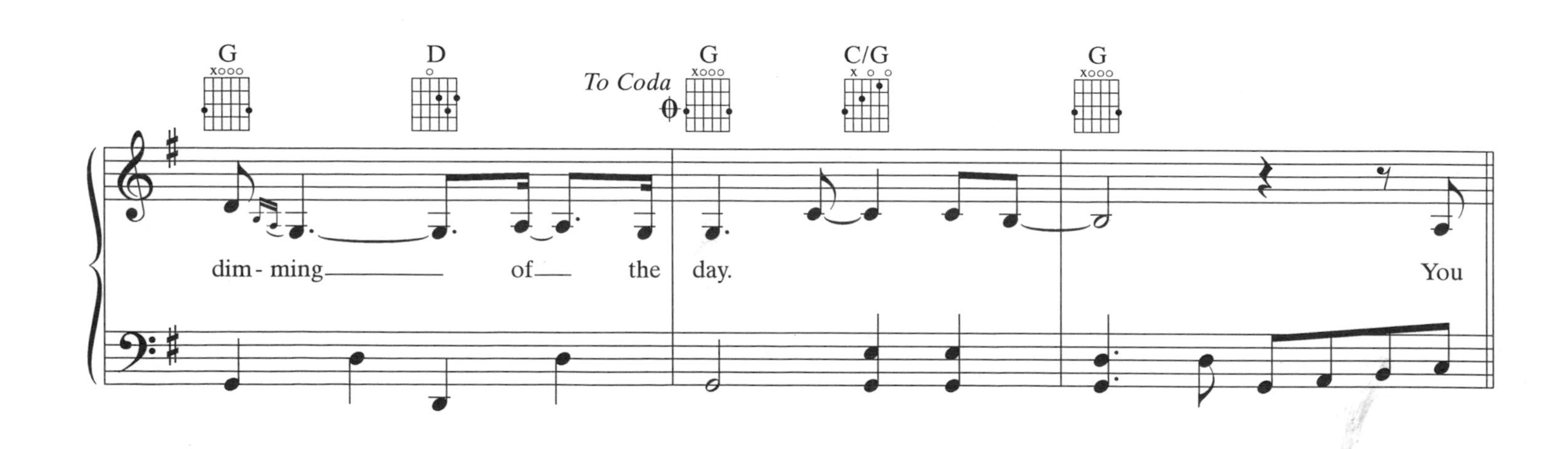
G
D
To Coda
G
C/G
G
dim-ming of the day. You

Chorus
D
pulled me like the moon pulls on the

A
D
tide. You know just where I

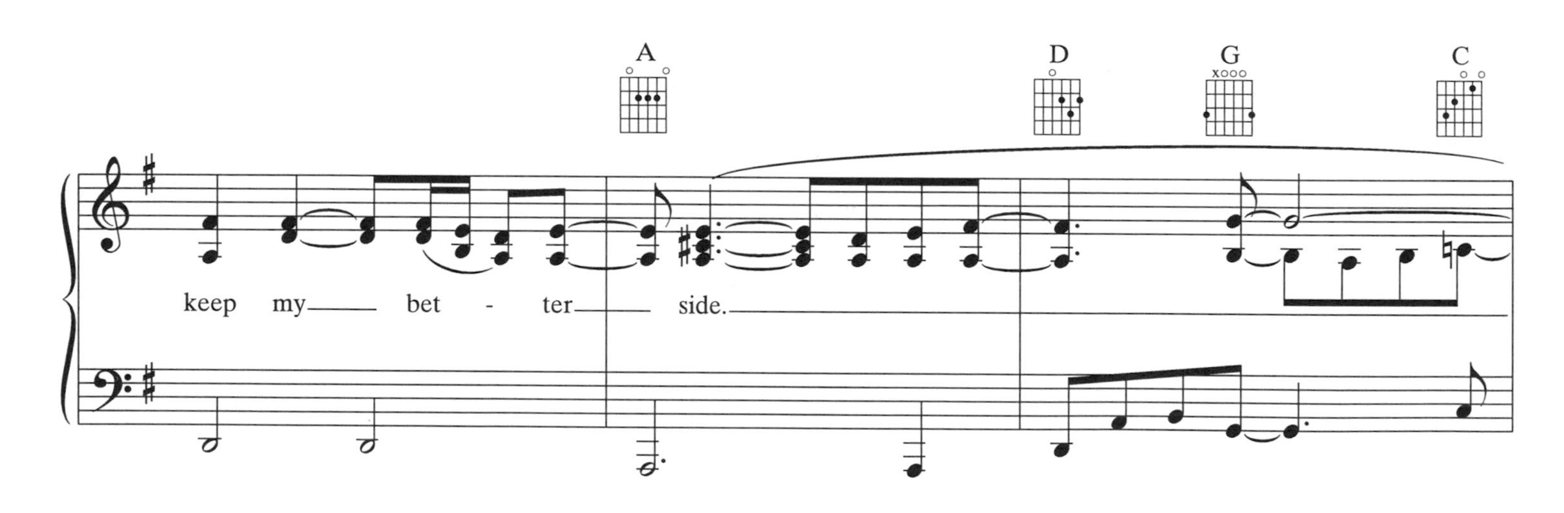
A
D
G
C
keep my bet - ter side.

1.
2.
D.S. al Coda
2.What days
3. I

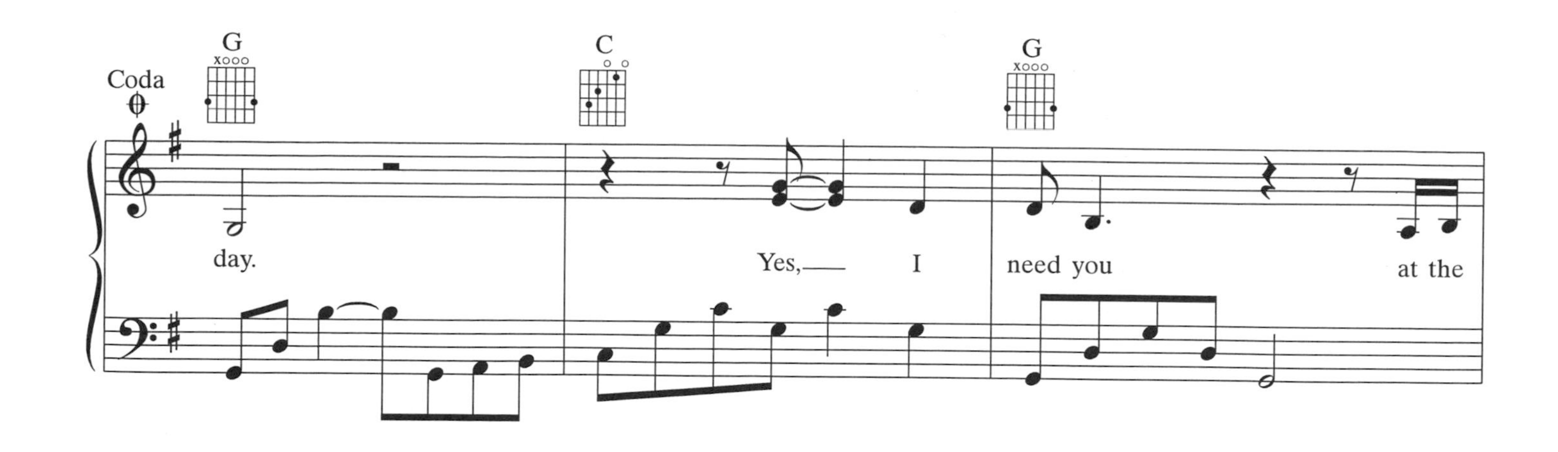

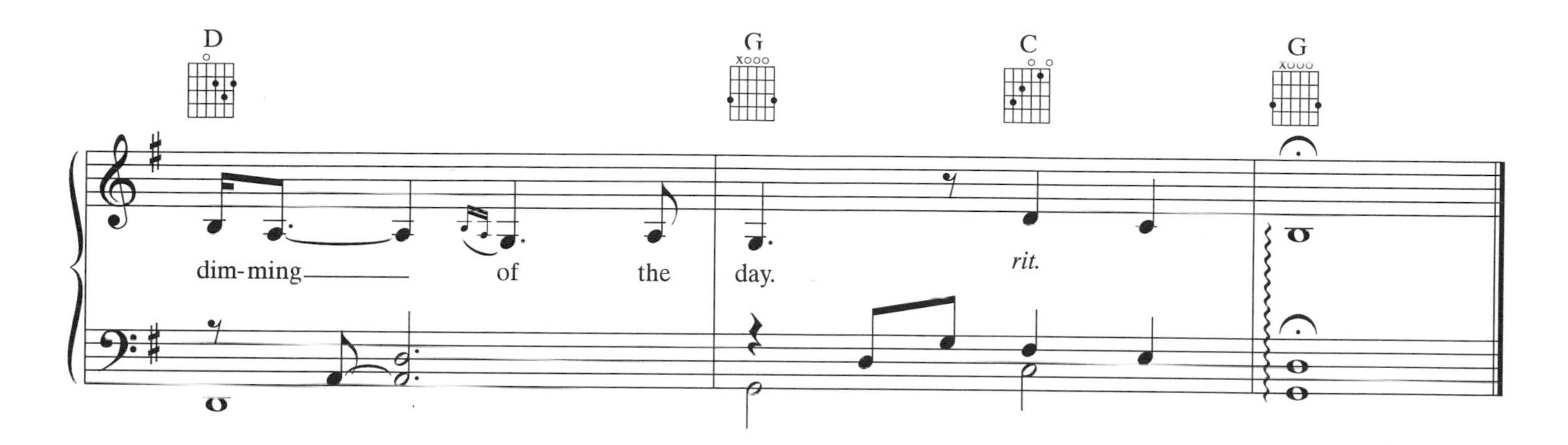

Additional Lyrics

2. What days have come to keep us far apart,
   A broken promise or a broken heart?
   Now all the bonny birds have wheeled away;
   I need you at the dimming of the day.

   2nd Chorus:
   Come the night, you're only what I want;
   Come the night, you could be my confidant.

3. I see you on the street and in company;
   Why don't you come and ease your mind with me?
   I'm living for the night we steal away;
   I need you at the dimming of the day.
   Yes, I need you at the dimming of the day.

FEELING OF FALLING

Dsus2/F♯
Gsus2
A5
C5
3fr.
D5
mind, it gets too wor - ried, and I just can't get no
F♯m7
Dsus2
rest, oh ba - by, oh,
cresc. poco a poco
Moderately, with a beat
C
A
A7(no3rd)
2fr.
that's when I call you up in - stead.
D/A
A
A7(no3rd)
2fr.
D/A

A
D
1. Af - ter mid - night, ba - by,
2. See additional lyrics
mf
sit - tin' here all a - lone.
I tried to call your num - ber, ba - by,
but you weren't at home.

A
D
I been a good girl, ba - by,
I'm through with all that mess.
Esus4
F♯m7
But the way I'm feel - in' right now, dar - lin',
G6/9
you know, it scares me half to death. And I miss that feel - in'

Chorus
Am7
C/D
3fr.
G/D
D
F♯m7
of fall -
G6/9
Am7
C/D
3fr.
G/D
D
in' on o - ver the ledge.
F♯m7
1.
G6/9
To Coda
2.
G6/9
D.S. al Coda
Coda
G6/9
A
3. It ain't some-thing you get o - ver;

D
A
D
you might think you made it through.
A
D
You can turn your head and walk a - way, ba - by,
A
D
but it nev - er takes its eyes off o' you.
A
D
It - 'll push your foot right through the floor- board, ba - by,

A
D
make you cut them stream - ers down his back.
A
D
You waste what's pre- cious and you can't af- ford;
A
D
it runs your life right off the track.
A
Bm7
It keeps you boil - in' in that poi - son on - ly the

Additional Lyrics

2. That summer night in Texas, baby,
   Too hot and wet to sleep.
   I heard you pull up in the distance;
   You're comin' to get me relief.
   We went screamin' down the highway, baby,
   So much faster than we should.
   You pulled me over in the moonlight;
   Man, I still can feel that hood.

   2nd Chorus:
   And I miss that feeling.
   I wanna fall on over the ledge.
   When that rain starts falling,
   I want to take a real good look at that ledge.

STEAL YOUR HEART AWAY

Words and Music by
Paul Brady

G/A
3fr.
A7
I know this rhy - thm we been mov - ing to is way too
But that don't mat - ter to a lov - er with a rest - less heart,
Dsus2/A
slow, babe.
no, babe.
'Cause
G/A
3fr.
A7
Each time our bod - ies are sup - posed to meet,
you still want to wake up to a dif - fer - ent scene,

Gmaj9/A
2fr.
A7sus4
well, I'm here still missing a beat.
some screen gem like the one in your dream,
G/A
3fr.
A7
And when I look at you I see in your eyes we're still
and leave me stand-ing like a fool in the wings, still
A/B
Bm7
G/A
3fr.
danc-ing to a dif-f'rent tune.
wait-ing for a part to play.

D
A
Take me to your dream - ing place and
D/F♯
A/E
D
G/A
3fr.
o - pen up my eyes.
Let me see what it
Bm7
Em7
takes to be your lov - er in dis - guise.
Show me how I do those things that

D/F♯
A/E
D
G/A
3fr.
D/F♯
A
make you want to stay
'cause I'll go cra - zy if
Bm7
A
D/F♯
Bm7
Em7
I don't find
the words I got - ta say
G/A
3fr.
1.
Bm
D/F♯
F♯m7
Gsus2
to steal your heart a - way.
(Steal your heart
D/A
A
Bm
D/F♯
F♯m7
Gsus2
a - way.
Steal your heart.)

2.
Bm
Em7
I can't
(Steal your heart a - way.)
G/A
3fr.
Fsus2
wait an - oth - er day.
I can't
Gsus2
Fsus2
wait for you.
Don't make me wait.
C/D
D
1. I

Additional Lyrics for fade

2. And maybe you think that it's alright
   To leave me waiting every night,
   To put me down in company
   In front of everyone we see,
   To take my loving when it's free,
   And then to throw it back at me.
   Well baby, I just can't stand it.

3. 'Cause I can be the one for you,
   And I can make your dreams come true.
   And I can love you like she can,
   'Cause fancy clothes don't make no woman.
   Believe me, baby,
   I got what it takes to make you feel good.

4. And maybe you think a girl should be
   As pefect as a girl can be,
   To love you when you're feeling down
   And miss you when you're not around.
   Well, I can't be that one for you;
   I can only be the one that loves you.

5. Hey,
   What's this on your mind?
   Hey, what's this change of mind?
   Hey, what's this on your mind?

STORM WARNING

Words and Music by
Terry Britten and Lea Maalfrid

G
A
To Coda
D
we may get tossed to-night.
Storm
G
Bm7
E/G♯
warn - ing,
he's made it
pret-ty plain
G
A
G/B
he's fall-in' for an - oth - er,
found a new lov -
A/C♯
D
er,
and he won't be back a - gain.
A
D
A
Can't stop a
riv - er
when it's burst its

D
G
A
banks.
I've seen the look in his eyes;
G/B
A/C♯
he's in love and hyp - no - tized.
D/F♯
G
Bm7
Time of mourn - ing, There's al - read - y
E/G♯
G
A
been a flood of my tears. Such a sense of loss to - night.
G/B
A/C♯
D
Nought to do but ride it out.
3

G
A/C♯
D
D/F♯
G
D
G
A/C♯
D
D/F♯
G
A
D
Can't stop a riv - er
A
D
G
when it's burst its banks.
I won - der how
A
G/B
A/C♯
D.S. al Coda
long it's gon - na take
to get o - ver this
heart - break.

Coda
D
G
Bm7
E/G♯
G
A
G/B
1.2.
A/C♯
3.
A/C♯
D
dim. poco a poco
pp

HELL TO PAY

Words by Bonnie Raitt
Music by Randy Jacobs and Bonnie Raitt
Moderately fast
C♯m7
4fr.
mp
C♯m7
4fr.
1. Hey mis - ter, we want you to know__ we think you've tak - en this a -
F♯7
bout as far as it can go.___ It's a - bout to blow.-

C♯m7
4fr.
G♯m7♯5
You've got no- where to run; why don't you
sit back and watch the show?
2. You used to
𝄋
drop your lit - tle dar- lin' off at Sun- day School; fam-'ly val- ues while you're
3.4.5. See additional lyrics
mf
F♯7
get- tin' some be- hind the pool.
She's no - bod-y's fool.

C♯m7
4fr.
To Coda
G♯m7♯5
4fr.
Don't all be act- ing sur- prised when your
daugh-ter wants it bad as you.
1.2.
3.
Bridge
E
Well, you know times are hard, ain't it a bitch; but
F♯
the Jap - a - nese are mak- in' you twitch.
E
All your in- vest- ments are

F♯
G♯
4fr.
D.S. al Coda
turn-in' sour;
a-kind-a spoils your hap-py hour.
Coda
G♯m7♯5
4fr.
way it looks from here you won't have to wait; the
way it looks from here, no need to hes-i-tate. Have a par - ty,
cel - e- brate. The way it looks from here, won't have to wait for hell

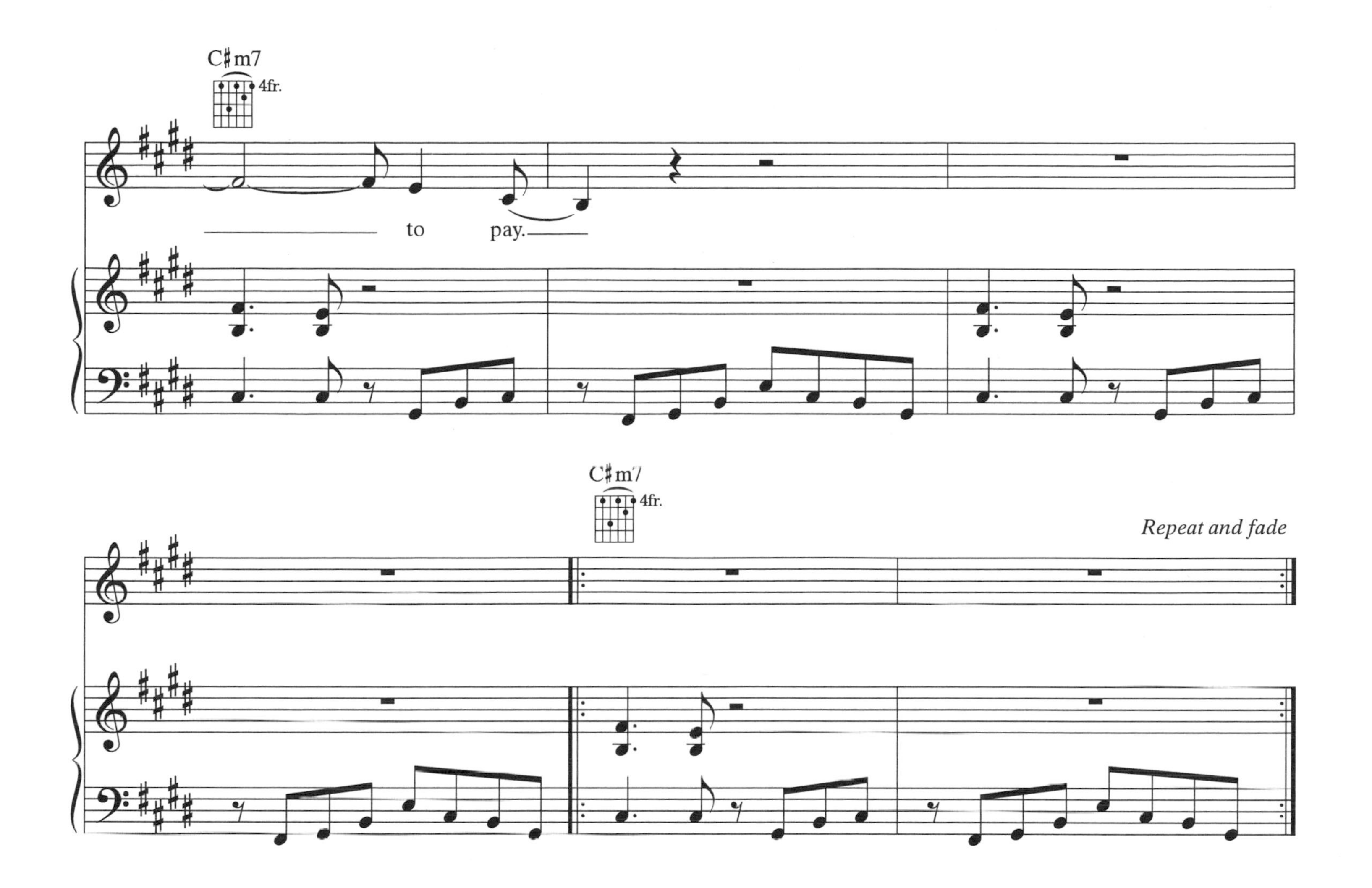

Additional Lyrics

3. *Instrumental*

4. You jack up the rent, you call in a loan;
   Clear your intent is to screw 'em out of all they own.
   Throw the dog a bone.
   Well, you'll be cryin' for mercy
   When your karma calls you on the phone. *(To Bridge)*

5. Look around, we're comin' your way;
   It's a wonder to us how you ever thought you'd get away.
   What you say...
   Well, the way it looks from here, *etc.*

SHADOW OF DOUBT

Words and Music by
Gary Nicholson

* Recorded a half step lower.

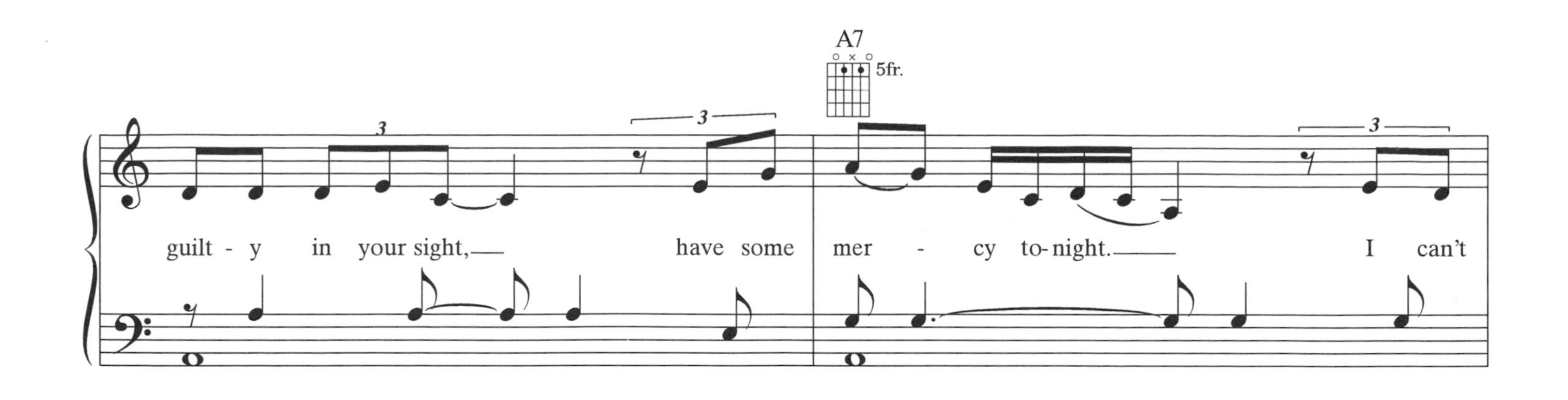
A7
5fr.
3
3
3
guilt - y in your sight,
have some
mer - cy to-night.
I can't

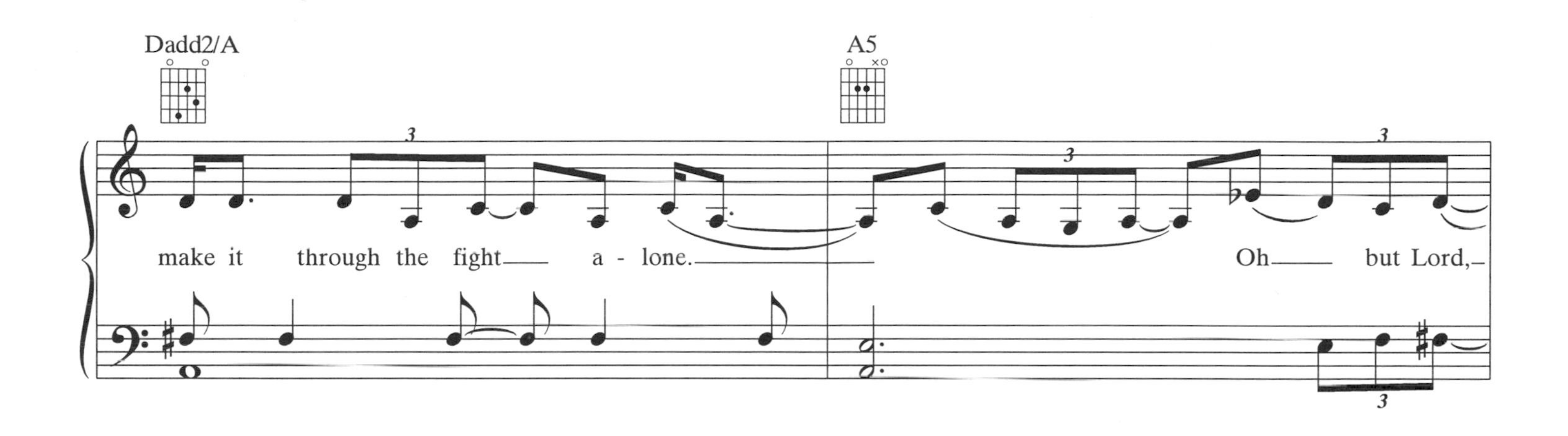
Dadd2/A
A5
3
3
3
3
make it through the fight a - lone.
Oh but Lord,

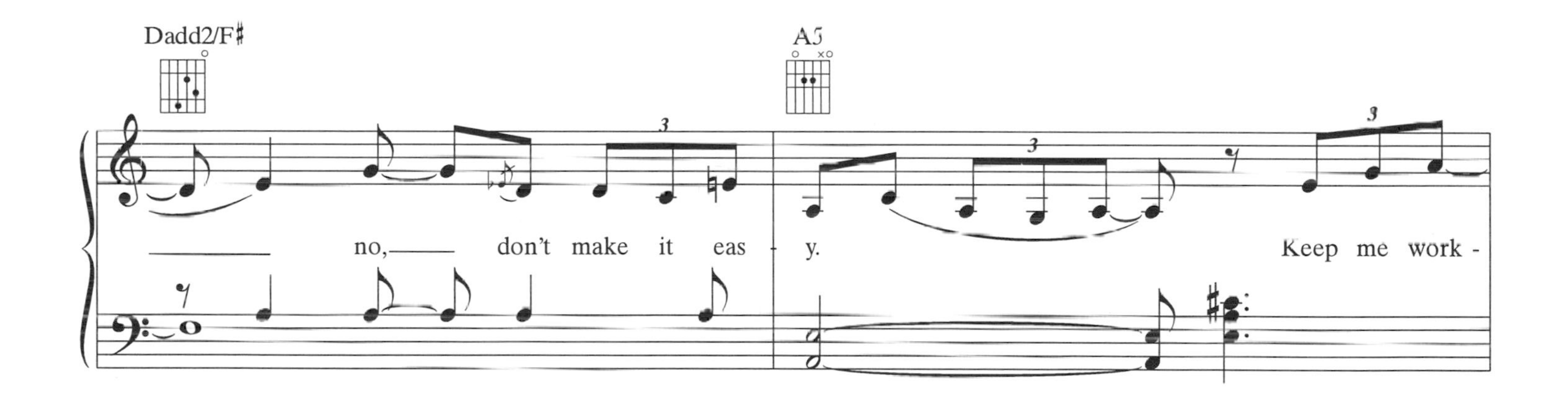
Dadd2/F♯
A5
3
3
3
no, don't make it eas - y.
Keep me work -

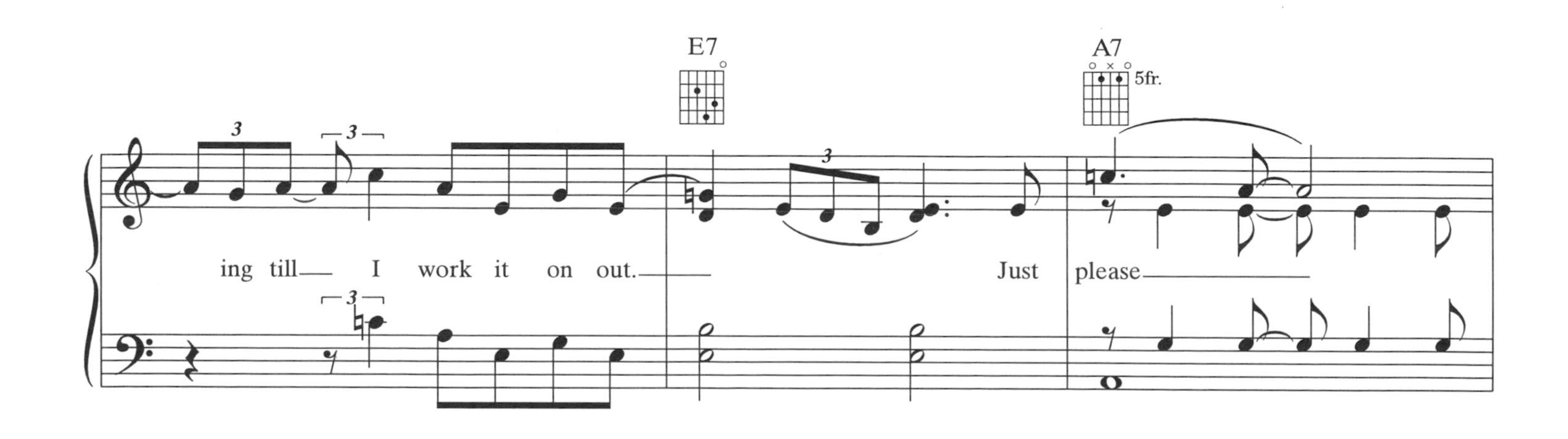
E7
A7
5fr.
3
3
3
3
ing till I work it on out.
Just
please

A
A°7
E7
shine e-nough light on me, till I'm
free from this shad-ow of doubt.
A5
Dadd2/A
E7
Keep me out of
the shad-ow of
A5
D
Am/C
doubt.
A5
1.2.
D
Am/C
2. As I

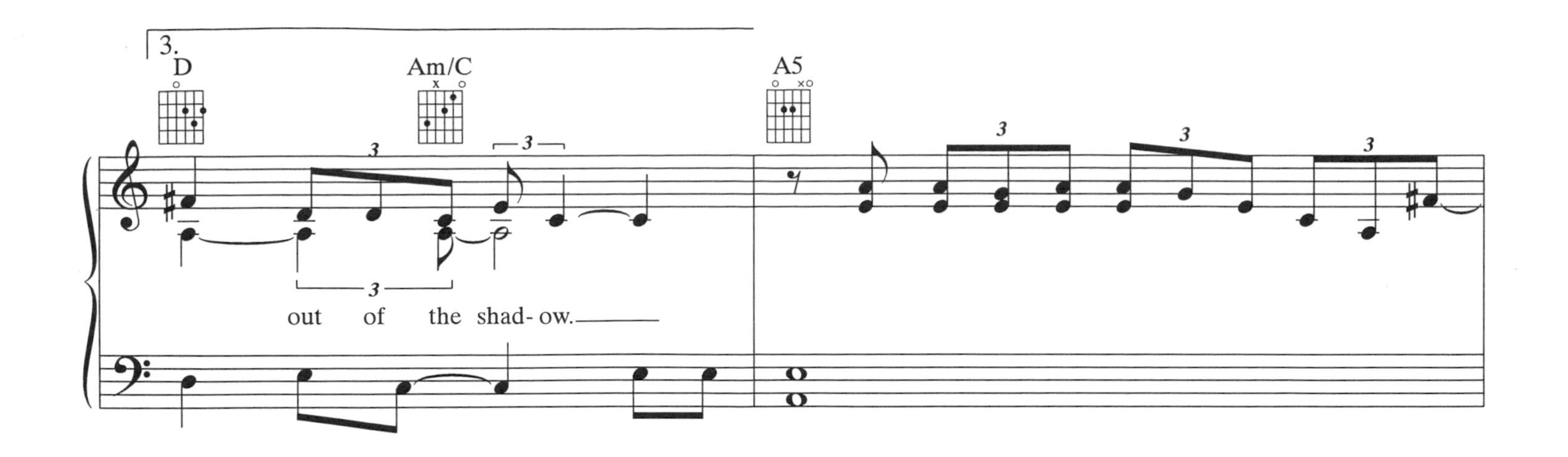

Additional Lyrics

2. As I try to make some sense of this world I'm up against,
   Well, I know my best defense is your love.
   When the struggle gets insane,
   And the lessons full of pain,
   Keep me calling out your name with love.
   Oh but Lord, no don't make it easy;
   Keep me workin' till I work it on out.
   Just please, won't you shine enough light on me
   Till I'm free from this shadow of doubt?
   Keep me out of the shadow of doubt.

3. Well, I whisper in the dark from the bottom of heart,
   And I'm searchin' for one star to shine.
   I will shout from mountain high,
   And I'll reach into the sky,
   Till you open up my eyes so blind.
   Oh but Lord, no, don't make it easy;
   Keep me workin' till I work it on out.
   Just please, please shine enough light on me
   Till I'm free from this shadow of doubt.
   Keep me out of the shadow, out of the shadow.